# THE PORTAGE POETRY SERIES

# SERIES TITLES

*The Underdream*
Aiyana Masla

*Wildfire*
Corie Rosen

*Pandora's Prairie*
Katherine Hoerth

*How We Argue*
Sharon Rose-Kourous

*The Weather of Our Names*
Cal Freeman

*Temporary Shelters*
Grant Clauser

*An Introduction to Error*
Deirdre Lockwood

*tic tic tic*
Heidi Seaborn

*And the Heart Will Not Quicken*
Russell Thorburn

*Lost Cathedral*
Hannah Rodabaugh

*Exile Is Home*
Elvis Alves

*Even the Sky*
Kevin Thomason

*Dining on Salt: Four Seasons of Septets*
Wayne Lee

*Torrential*
Jayne Marek

*Users with Access: New and Selected Poems*
Brandon Krieg

*Flu Season*
Katie Kalisz

*No Trouble Staying Awake*
Teresa Scollon

*Another Native Tongue*
Susan Riley Clarke

*Dear Lo*
Brady Bove

*Sadness of the Apex Predator*
Dion O'Reilly

*Do Not Feed the Animal*
Hikari Miya

*The Watching Sky*
Judy Brackett Crowe

*Let It Be Told in a Single Breath*
Russell Thorburn

*The Blue Divide*
Linda Nemec Foster

*Lake, River, Mountain*
Mark B. Hamilton

*Talking Diamonds*
Linda Nemec Foster

*Poetic People Power*
Tara Bracco (ed.)

*The Green Vault Heist*
David Salner

*There is a Corner of Someplace Else*
Camden Michael Jones

*Everything Waits*
Jonathan Graham

*We Are Reckless*
Christy Prahl

*Always a Body*
Molly Fuller

*Bowed As If Laden With Snow*
Megan Wildhood

*Silent Letter*
Gail Hanlon

*New Wilderness*
Jenifer DeBellis

*Fulgurite*
Catherine Kyle

*The Body Is Burden and Delight*
Sharon White

*Bone Country*
Linda Nemec Foster

*Not Just the Fire*
R.B. Simon

*Monarch*
Heather Bourbeau

*The Walk to Cefalù*
Lynne Viti

*The Found Object Imagines a Life: New and Selected Poems*
Mary Catherine Harper

*Naming the Ghost*
Emily Hockaday

*Mourning*
Dokubo Melford Goodhead

*Messengers of the Gods: New and Selected Poems*
Kathryn Gahl

*After the 8-Ball*
Colleen Alles

*Careful Cartography*
Devon Bohm

*Broken On the Wheel*
Barbara Costas-Biggs

*Sparks and Disperses*
Cathleen Cohen

*Holding My Selves Together: New and Selected Poems*
Margaret Rozga

*Lost and Found Departments*
Heather Dubrow

*Marginal Notes*
Alfonso Brezmes

*The Almost-Children*
Cassondra Windwalker

*Meditations of a Beast*
Kristine Ong Muslim

PRAISE FOR

# THE UNDERDREAM

Infused with grief, astonishment, and even a quiet joy, Aiyana Masla's profoundly humane imagination makes meaning amidst the misfortune of an intractable illness. Her delicately observed poems bring readers into the intimate spaces and hard places where tenderness coexists with pain, revealing the sensual details of an interior life. *The Underdream* held me within its spell from the first to the last line. Her words shimmer and sing.

—HOLLY WREN SPAULDING
author of *If August* and *Familiars*

*The Underdream* reckons remarkably with being strong and soft, fragile and forever. It's a book to turn to again and again, untangling and discovering new poems that feel like home. Masla molds language to her purpose, playing with words and syntax in ways that are at once captivating, innovative, and grounded. *The Underdream* belongs with all of us as we navigate the pain and joys of being mortal.

—LARKIN CHRISTIE
author of *gather all your supple creatures*

In *The Underdream*, Aiyana Masla deftly weaves together the personal intimacies of illness with global climate catastrophe and a deep love of the natural world. This book is at once quiet, in the hours of hospital stays, diagnosis and care, and loud, demanding its readers to look death in the face, to hold their own mortality, not apart from, but inextricably interwoven with the world around them.

—GRAY DAVIDSON CARROLL
author of *Waterfall of Thanks*

Aiyana Masla's poems are delicate, strong, and speak directly of the body—her own, the earth's. Her poems take on the rhythm of healing, intermittently uptempo, throbbing with renewal. As I did, you will root for this thoughtful, poised, determined poet as she finds her way through her own dark night, as she makes *surviving an act of imagination.* This illness, facing death, changes her. Everything is changed—the world around her, her connections to a street in her neighborhood, a tree, her family, her lover. She has done the impossible: *to be unimportant / & to be alive. Listen; / song upon song upon song is here.* This poet is slowly filling again with life. Sometimes woefully, sometimes joyfully, in her poems Aiyana sings our shared humanity.

—JEANNE M. LIGHTFOOT
author of *The Bones of It*

*The Underdream* is a slow, gentle kiss from a warm mouth in the cold. It conjures the other side; we survive, we remain, and we return. For those who have been so lucky to have avoided the world of medicine, waiting, fear, and stilted days, these poems will attune you with breathy attention to each precise moment of whatever exquisite, delicious, stinky, sticky time you have left in your joyful body. Earthy and earthly, this collection of poems will make you want to lick something, smell something, kiss someone, and pull in air to your lungs until they're so full they hurt.

—SOPHIE WOOD
author of *The Distance* and *After*

*The Underdream* offers a love fierce in its softness. Aiyana Masala welcomes us into an ocean of gratitude, and I am grateful to swim dizzy in its infinite. Here is an invitation into stillness. Here are all the colors of unhurried. Find yourself learning softness in the music of this collection, where acceptance and tiny slices of humor unfold in *griefjoy.* Meditations in these pages goosebump you through a *kaleidoscope* of earthy delights while time slows. Let these poems drizzle you in the honey of being alive, despite.

—FATIMA HIRSI
author of *Dreams for Earth* and *Everything Good is Dying*

# The Underdream

poems

Aiyana Masla

CORNERSTONE PRESS
UNIVERSITY OF WISCONSIN-STEVENS POINT

Cornerstone Press, Stevens Point, Wisconsin 54481
Copyright © 2025 Aiyana Masla
www.uwsp.edu/cornerstone

Printed in the United States of America.

Library of Congress Control Number: 2025940340
ISBN: 978-1-968148-06-5

Cornerstone Press titles are produced in courses and internships offered by the Department of English at the University of Wisconsin–Stevens Point.

DIRECTOR & PUBLISHER
Dr. Ross K. Tangedal

EXECUTIVE EDITORS
Jeff Snowbarger, Freesia McKee

EDITORIAL DIRECTOR
Brett Hill

SENIOR EDITORS
Paige Biever, Eva Nielsen, Reilly Crous

PRESS STAFF
Lilly Kulbeck, Aja Wolley, Sophie McPherson, Sam Bjork, Madison Schultz, Autumn Vine, Allison Lange

*to you,*
*who is alive*
*right now*

# CONTENTS

## I. NIGHT

## II. BETWEEN ROOMS

## III. THAW

*I cannot tell if the day
is ending, or the world, or if
the secret of secrets is inside me again*

—Anna Akhmatova

# I. NIGHT

# Green

green began the foggiest dawn
long lashes           or just legs
new sun         on dew       two legs
blink,                    rub together
     where honey was every
morning for a thank you
just my two legs,
hairy, furred
after a loose dress. For the
I grow hair, still
edge & *I am needled*
left hand's vein         thinking *no!*
resilience, about an hour     no day is
waisted
our just a little
blood                  kicking tender
hands in the morning
blanketed, as time swelled, as evening
bruised, tea from roots      & slowly

loosened, wings spluttering, lifted

I've come to show you
healing at the time of a buzz of peepers
    my dug up
time taking its August
entropy, always
then night. If there is joy
days that touched      swept by
              a clean grief — it was those leaf wings
an exposed, ferny unfurl
that small honey          & never was my fault.
A week now I
sat here in         the softest moss, wrapped
soft grass          round my own face & sat

in front                in the same
mouth                   prayer tree
putting on dew          sun, dark
cricket green           a ceremony then, like on the page
spruce I remember                about joy
so still                         in it. Even
gentleness                       gentleness
I remember the groundbloom of trout lilies
returning over life.

# Clinic

Pressed between four gray walls
is the endless waiting room.
No windows, sterile air
& no sun.
Dry & defeated under
neon blinking, slumped in hard
cold plastic chairs. Still alive,
we humans stink -
shame, sanitizer, nausea, foreboding.
An exhausted sermon, time heaves its weight.
Morning's time, yet heavy, unrested
the too-clean-scrubbed white of the tiles.
Familiar, flat infomercials, medical & captioned
on the mounted tv
running their silent flashing. The invasive high pitch
of life machines, temperature checks, blood pressure
& X-ray cameras, needles, bulky pills
air purifiers & stethoscopes. Months pass, days tighten.
Doors shut, open, shut, squeak on the paled linoleum.
Hushed, careful voices,
the metal sound of the scale,
whisper - mutter
(the way people talk
when they only half-want you
not to hear), voices clip board stiff, & tense,
                    *she's still too thin —*

while outside, June.          Robust,     pulsing.

## Empty Empty

In the afternoon, high above, the winter sparrows
tear at thick white clouds with their beaks
                             & call

until some small sunlight
comes, a hole in the sky the size of a bird's mouth

exposed    expanse
of empty       empty

but the sparrows keep calling
not quite a song, not quite a song
               make the light come down.

# Before

the street was bare
>        except for bite-wind
to walk against

heart racing
>        legs aching
with effort, teeth.

A discarded take out container's silver glint
& grease, half an empty Corona
leaning against a battered stoop.
Rattle   of iron gate lock
on iron gate.
It was frozen-bugger cold.
Numb fingered & skinny
with disease.

A cough that tore the morning.
A cough that brought up blood.

Tremble-edged
crunching plastic, stepped on cigarette
ash cold cement & a large hole
>        shaped like a damp purple ribbon, a cinched knot
growing cavernous     between shadow, lung, & road.

Broken-glass-city,                    rasping,           shuttered.

Look, before, & see her
limp up hill
with not much left
patience, infinity, or faith —

mornings like that, repair seemed inconceivable.

## Inside

Sit    in the slant        of light
that fills this room


weep        two cups
                    of tea



long
fold
me            in bright colors.



I am not dead.



I am learning        softness
I am dreaming        time.



Come.

# Glimmerers

i. Boiling eggs clink together in hot water.

ii. Your face, pulling close. Plum jam, beet juice
& melted butter running purple down my fingers,
leaving a streaky stain on your chin, neck.
Sticking breath, gray owl, grasshopper,
yellow trees, evening. Slow dancing
with you to the sound of crickets.

iii. A body decaying. A body to protect.

iv. My want, I am not afraid of you. Not naive
that I won't lose you, either. You sit
by my thin legs extended under the heavy blanket.
Your hand rests on my knee. The place that bends.
You are facing the window.
I watch your back as you breathe.

v. You take care of me. The window is open.

vi. Now I hold your warm hand.
Proud, closely, walk slow
along the town's main street.
We walk together, against all odds.

vii. Fire

viii. We are letting ourselves.

## In Late November

day white shards of morning shiver
                              through the partly open
                    windows, clean stale air

from each dulled room.
                              Sleeping, waking, sleeping
                    in half light

float
                    from the long
branch

upturned
                    half-
live sugar.

                    Then lifting,
          twirl
                    towards the dirt.


                    Untouched by rain
          for weeks
                    with painful slowness, become


                                             noon / decay /
                                             nourishment.

# This Bed

you stand to leave.
Our grip released, both
palms sweaty, unwind
this flesh riot map
repulsion. Veins,
wrist, shoulder, liver,
exposing gray hills
& shadow valleys. Descent
of watery, slimy yoke,
squeamish smell of sanitizer,
picked at medical tape,
& needled bruises. Inward blemish
my hip bone, a scissor tipped ledge
under the skin. Corrugated blood.
Little pathways that arch purple,
agitated yellow. Body,
the romance washed out. Mortal.
A loose strand of hair, lint, static.
I look up at you
let forward into worried
uncharted territory,
smell unknown red
wilderness in, out
the rough edges yield the softest parts.
Meeting & meeting, like waves & sand,
slipping / swooping / pulling back
an ugly tension — then loose
your smile, a kind of miracle.

## Patience

the only movement most days   flurry                windsweeps


                              twirling    the
                                              wide
                                       field.


& the birds in bare branches, perched

                                       sing silhouettes
                                       in shadowless trees

let softness fall on their feathers        un-complaining


& the sad light, unchanging since dawn


pours through on ruin, dazzles              blue,  silent.

# A Letter From My Left Arm

In the night, you were convincing enough.
This morning, relief of rain, tangled hair
I don't want to brush. Let me tell you
about stretching out, then, into the fresh, fragrant
after          driving & dangling my fingers
through an almost-warm wind. The open window,
as if summer — as if not sick — as if almost carefree,
half an hour. Abandon. As if able to forget
the daily prescription. Kidney yellow & chalk white,
plastic red.          In the pitch, mid-pinch, how we persist.
I could share with you rashed, inflamed places,
but not now. Now I am under a purple sweater,
half-asleep, watching the bored face of the Covid-screener.
She sits at a table by the double doors, half-heartedly
involved in a crossword puzzle on her phone. See
how irritated she is, interrupted by someone coming in, "Any
feverorchills?cough?shortnessofbreathordifficultybreathing?
newlossoftasteorsmell? sorethroat?muscleorbodyaches?
nauseaorvomiting?fatigue?diarrhea?headaches?"
Who doesn't have a headache today?
I am stunned as people pass ahead of me,
enter by shaking their heads,    nah. nope. No, no thank you.
We each lie, a little. Single file, move into the lab.
I wait in the gray seat     closest to the closed window.
Number 044 is called
& Laura-or-Clair approaches. Familiar in clogs,
mint green smocked, & masked.
Daily, I visit her glossy rooms. How well I know
the measure of her steps. Her stride. Her bulk.
Let me show you how she remembers my birthdate!
See, how she no longer asks the spelling of my last name?
She has my address memorized. Please. Understand!
Know of our strange intimacies.
I will take you to the sticky chair,
where she traces what was tenderness

with a soaked cotton ball, the same gesture each time.
Almost lulling, the predictability of our ritual.
I'd like to rest on you here, let you muffle
her cheap joke about sanitizer. Let you soften
the harsh, beeping overhead lights. Let you quiet
the high-pitched motions of Laura-or-Clair, I always
confuse their blond, bowed heads. When I'm more lucid,
I can tell them apart by looking for which one
has the *I HATE PEOPLE* pin with the dog on it.
Can you hear her nasal lilt? I want to stay underneath
my sweater. Will you do this for me, just today?
Joking again as she everyday probes & pokes
the softest underside, the round, concave middle shape of me,
searching for my hiding-vein.
Now I fake laugh, now I hope that she can't tell
it's a fake laugh. Sting of rubbing alcohol, a sharpness.
I'll tell you the truth:
you can only yield to so much familiar.
Soft slap. Prick again, new digging. Laura-or-Clair makes small tal
while she pulls, flattens, tapes, sterilizes & I blink back,
throating poison & bitter. Shucking sincerity, prepared
to trust science over my skin.    See Laura-or-Clair
complaining now, eye rolling & pantomiming body language
from the line at Starbucks; slouching, then cocking her head,
as if listening for her name, her latte order being called.
I don't watch, turn away & look instead at the sterile wall,
painted pill blue, patient as she takes my depths to measure.
Shaky, unleveled, there is a last time for everything, I think —
for Laura-or-Clair's chatter, for warm, syrupy small talk between us
for their butterfly needles & mundane stories
about waiting in line for coffee.  For anything.
Laura-or-Clair commenting on the weather
while she pulls, flattens, tapes, sterilizes, & I blink
you, lightheaded
you, clasped
close, death.

# Sleep

in blurry ice & a pale
wide swamp.

Sleep in a room with no door.

Dissolve in a secret heat.

Feed on gusts

on hardened, naked branches.

Swallow.

Sustain salted, early day
stretching on                    & on.

Let quiet lay
like a blanket,

like snow
or another body,

protecting

like the word, "no."

# Flicker

flickering out the window
a memory-shadow

of a slim red pine
bending in a blond field

shimmer illness
weedy dusk

how good it is now,
ringing a cape of bells

crossing goldenrod stalks
& milkweed husks

scarring cold topsoil,
reaching down

underneath evening.
Winter's constellation

draws water, rings
sound that sparkles.

# Want

Day-want, night-want
on & on
black night, blue blue day.

Bruises of leaving & arriving
& leaving
parted places between the trees.

Want
the smell of dirt, fingers, grass stains
tired arms, quiver thighs, fresh cut, bee sting.

Want a haircut, a scar. Suntan,
a tattoo. Fresh lipstick. Snap
of an old way, finally breaking. Want

the sound of a door closing,
a door opening.
Creak of change. Into another room.

Moon. Sound of new dawn, yellow dawn
up   up   up
not when this, or with that, not then, or if

but here, as it is. A body,
& alive. Morning again.
Same body, same room.

Same wall & same chip in the ceiling.
The moment turned over, belly up, up, up,
face turned to face it

vulnerable, unguarded
bristle
          hollow
stunning.

## Luminous

Loose, loosened
those days, you were singed.
Drove alone
in the cold car, your hair
static, looking out the window
blowing hot breath
into your hands.
Wretched, immaculate
sadness gave
way to a blaze
that broke your golden
falling, you
charred, you burnt
red at the end
spilled yellow shimmer
a stark blue barely holding
you up, your wind
whispered generous about
to lay bare the sky.
Scars, that secret
you ached & ached
in our chests
pounded days & days
against the muted pavement.
Valley, silent highway
dipping down
into the sweet night
of endings.

# Savored

Near the empty soccer field, with its wide shoulders
the pink day fading, every beech & maple lit
husky purple & dim dusk swept feathery blankets over the
streets.
You pulled the car over, stepped into the smell of frost
shivering clean sips of paper-thin moonlight.
Humming pickup, thudding Volvo,
flash of teeth & thrum of radio bass.
You crossed & stood
alone in the dry meridian
picked a small marigold, planted by the town department
glowing secret in the quickening night
burning elegy smell of cold pollen.
Two blinking stars, tiny petals
small fires in the blackness
your toes, cold
your breath, bitter in your mouth
the blossom, now crushed in your pocket
salty, a pollen stain you couldn't see,
but smelt. Small ceremony
you almost didn't stop for.

## Pain, My Body

is a mossy lake beneath quilts.   Cave, reserves & a gateway,
monochromatically green. Raw, large, unfolded,
dark soil leaf litter                cell by cell
emptying into an & .
There is the way          through, which is to say      the only

way through.
Oh, syrup maker. Oh, body. Denial is a latch.
Fastening, a hard fight.
Relinquish the edge, the body (smolder),
my body's indiscernible stab.
Through & through & through & this,
ferocious,        *renew, renew.*
You told me to be slow, thickening
mossy lake, cave
to let myself stink, sink, soft,          to let myself.
To be    decomposing soil.
                    To stay.
Smolder, then    scalding.  The gate, ajar.

# Encanto

A small rupture —

an opening that sings.

# II. BETWEEN ROOMS

# Glint

In the midst of everyone
silver quiver, a life.


You, dirt & glitter
after all
small, shining.

## I Am Not Ready, Yet

I will not say goodbye
not even on early mornings filling with steam, light
the thrill of my waking body. I couldn't yet, not yet
not yet I still have work to do it is not over neighborhoods
to get to know. I have to taste the ocean again, I still have to do
big more generous with joy     tell him the truth   Not yet
I want to hear her hearty laugh again & I want
to show my paintings to your mother It's not too late
fresh baking bread & lemons your breath sweet
from fruit juice you promised to take me
to that old restaurant in Red Hook with the jazz singer
in summer I want to watch you eat mussels marinara
hard laugh salt & cold water slap my thigh I am
not ready yet     Walk walk & walk until we're blistered Wind
also I might be terrified but the bathroom floor
isn't clean & the laundry basket is full I don't want you to be left
with the chores not yet I want the smell of the library
the sound of my boots in snow in a quiet forest
a poem knocking the breath out of me your weight
crushing me on the couch the print of pillow-cheek
in the morning cedar & coffee my family
together all together again
I am not ready Not Ready sun through the window
the kindness of strangers to run once more! Spontaneous
dancing     eyeliner there is too much to do yet still
to undo just rain   or a crowded pulsing room
where I have to shout to be heard
over sweaty thumping music. The streets full of us,
our shouting.         Don't let me forget
I want one more spring afternoon
& then another, another.
Perhaps that is where I will linger,
when I do become everything & nothing
dispersed.
In the soft, cloying air
of peonies   blooming.

# Joy in the Quiet Places

A not so glamorous & not so fiery day,
slipping between the grand folds of nothing,
pinging telephone, hissing radiator,
persistently humming fridge,
nearby buzz of traffic, siren & horn,
piling emails, the tea kettle boiling up hot air.

Then,                    the quiet place between songs,
when the record player whirs just dust

the shaft of afternoon, the winter chickadee,
the miracle of oranges in February,
the braided, superfluous tassel, hot pink —

& winter glints a golden sphere of hush
across the table, the hush of blossoms
in a round vase caught by light
reflects a shimmering circumference on the wood

lifting my shape to reach my hand in, to touch.
Dipping my fingers into fleeting
ethereal honey.

# Letter From My Lung To My Legs

For you the spider of my anatomy weaves
        a long distance
miles of bed & day between us.

For you I am willing.
        When you fear - swell,
for you I allow

the risk of chaos
        or ritual entering every
where, griefjoy reaching you

panging, iridescent
        & moments
later, wet.

I can't help the needles, the pills, the sirens —
        don't mind them. They will split you.
They will open.

You strong, scarred, bright blooms
        you uncategorizable limbs
what doesn't move through you in full chroma?

*

*

I wish we could tolerate the nighttime
        without the twitch of leaping nerves.
I wish the morning coolness to goosebump you fresh.

Catastrophe of color which blurs up & down the hill
        for you, the wind gathering petals of skirts, my easy
pleasure-wish for us. We are so similar — see it?

& one day, you
         will be my home to home,
that tend, that closer.

I'd like to, then, threading, be the kissed hush
         be yours, winged & whole. Concave the sky into clean sound
fingerprints of sleep, a loyal blue.

# A Time

she spoke of witches
her lips got wet as she talked
her hands excited

hill of tree fingers
we, rolling all the way down
sticks caught in our hair

# Greywater

somehow, shiny dimness.
My second winter in bed with the windows open

         sparks

day's heartbeat of cold air
comes through a lucky number
winded, silver afternoons.


Is it strange to thank a sickness?


It cuts into a life, burrows into a body,
performs havoc, kills.


Thumps repeated, long hours
in the windowless clinic,
pushes side effects, night terrors,
harsh daily swallows of chemical pills.
Steals pleasure; radiation, intervention, surgical knives,
suffocating  medical schedules,    hot & secret tears.
Weakens even  stern doctors.
Cancels plans, loses jobs, loses blood,  isolates, insulates
kills us

      scars
   sharpens
anxiety upon anxiety


forces absurd hours prone, yielded.


Is it strange? Sickness, who draws fluid & fear
cuts away & closes in
with stress, & fatigue, chronic with terror


empties & emptied
    presses tight into tight stomachs the mystery of surviving


drags pain through this year,     & the next.

Who, grotesque & shocking, has left so many
without a bearable way.
Is it strange that its reflection glitters
river bed cold, thaw of ice?

Sickness that flattened & laid bare
those whirring, dizzied, sloppy days         of my attempts

slowed what wouldn't be slowed
worked & re-worked resilience
made family of friends & lover
made surviving an act of imagination —

is it strange to thank this sickness?
Repatterned, returned, renewed, & therefore,

                                    a life.

# Daybed

in between leaving & leaving
I walk into sky, open mouthed.

I love what I love.

The firm breasts of the hill
the hum & hover & swell of night.
Condensation as it widens morning
no-end pavement, winded pink.

The effervescent touch
of, finally,              not numbness

unhindered, sanguine
& unreproaching

each   other / this   instant
fleeting / exquisite.

Solaced

in the quickening glow

the day-meadow

with its bed-head hair


you face me

your wet mouth

almost laughing

# From a Still Place

Lit, falling
      the   petals
              from early      tulips
once in a jar
      in the kitchen
            now tumbled red
across the counter,
table, floorboards.
Red O's on fire
      we kept as long as we could, now
curl, drift, scatter         sca t te  r         & flash
little dramatic deaths   in springtime.

        Spring        time,        gasp / eternity

of thick birdsong, supple hours, cold wind, warming sun
rays reflected
in small brown bottles
of root-tonic, gifted
& lining the uncleaned,
cluttered sink. From underneath blue Afghan weight, dream
water-songs. Whisper, mumble, murmur, thirst. In fever,
         all that appears to be taken
         is still here.

To be given
such a gift. To be given
      another chance

## Walking Edges

Lift,  carry          fiber                         fragile-seeming bones

                  ferns & brush.                    Shift from
        arches

 big toe scraping                                   lichen mud

maple seed, pine sap        pricker catch

                           arm swing              bend

weary,   lean                     in breath, creek gurgle

afternoon through branches

                 blushing light.

Returned, April's long dusk.

                 So close to lost

having faltered   a hard, vast winter.                & yet.

            To rest, here,    is not to lose.

The foot tastes darkness

        through the boot, its medicine

unmistakably rich & palpable.

# & After

we are quiet
mouths full of quiet
our bodies
stones in a river

bed, shimmer

all of it undone
our simplest desires.

# This Practice

These mornings
cobalt cave gleamed, spring cream lavendered
wild mustard, chartreuse.
Long, the return from night
scarlet-reddened, opera rose
extended, magentaed ritual. Turquoise fool's
devoted gold, peach candy, opening
hands, slow as whispers, robin's egg.
Brushes, this unhurried bleed
the lamp's soft circle & room-warm tap water.
Canyon spreading, staining sleeves
wetted paper singing
an amaranthine smear where flyaways were tucked, ear
now charcoal mouthed. Splattered;
the tv tray used as an easel,
the rim of the flower vase used for washing
happy-marking the sheets of the bed
splashed & supple. Thickened with pigment,
tinted, these tender minutes
formed, pulsing, possible.
Wrists opaque, fingers saffron mystic ox, flax
swallowed in permanent green light.
Worry enveloped in ochre umber
submerged mars, burnt orange, manganese night siren
soaking through ancestor's dusk, purple ivory covered
wet coil black. Listening
as patient, vivid
as animate as soil.

# Being Ill

Laying still
has ripped open
a thin, temporal   levity

on a morning
it is snowing
my own worth revealed to me

again & again, again
an   incandescent   nothingness.

## The Ends

Tender me

scared

hurrying towards death;

frantic for un-frayed fabric

lusting after tight seams

the crease & the wrinkle-less

always

dreaming of DONE.

List crossed off neatly

pile folded, clean

the lint picked.

A finally satisfied smile at rest

on a contented face.

# Nowadays

Late, when sirens turn over the midnight
before it is swallowed purple
glowing, the streetlight
a perpetual, pretend moon.

Illness, that consuming mouth
its grief a noise rushing
over the minutes, a river.

Muffled dog bark, truck brakes
slow, low call of the bedsheets.

At first, the apartment was a safe cupboard
small boat in a wrecking storm.

If you lay flat on the floor        under the windows, no one
could see you from the street.
The hum not quite wind or water or fields
but something alive, like them, churning & breathing.

Now, the walls, skin, boundaries, borders
where the body ends & streets begin —
no longer blurred, no longer threatening.
A line has been drawn. Deep, thick, angled, sloping.

All is changed.

## Thankyou

small life in half darkness
tasting leaves,    sweeter sweet decay
as the swollen morning opens, parts
of myself. I have given every      one                over in sleep

to this healing, poetry the edge
of me, the only shape left hanging on my hollow
I try to braid as I braid long hair in the dark.
Just like my mother, I have longed to be

what I already am. This redness
a fire I've known better  with my fast tongue than
any other quickness.

Until this morning.
             I have been emptied.

What is left is thankyou. As I swallow & swallow
it brims my body with warmth, with salt
the most frustrating & forceful are elementally   submerged
underneath its eclipse.

I walk to the window, unsure of where to put my hands
now that I am oceans of thankyou. The pinkening hills.

My words survive as small dark seeds
& are buried.
             I have little to say.

# III. THAW

# The Impossible

I know how to lay
still in the curve of snow, a stone in a deep field
listen to the wide sky
infinite possibility, infinite yellow day


I know how to be cradled in its cold, soft lap
until it bleeds brightness into my skin & my toes sting
stretch time timeless


to be unimportant
& to be alive. Listen;
song upon song upon song is here.

# Reverence

Dim wet on everything
sheen           drip
                     drip
                     drip
leaning shards from night
in the green field
gasp, gleaming.


The sick woman,
out for her walk, early
down the driveway
gravel & mud
then back up it again


half an hour's time, enough.

# Dew & Dirt

Every morning, so far, I am alive.

Every morning, as if out of a thicket
or fog, the world returns, slowly seeping;
wets my skin with color. Life rushes in
messy & ordinary
swollen day pressed
against folds unfolding
such softness.

& to my surprise, my teeth are all
still in my mouth
small & sharp as last night.

Every morning, some living hunger, & birds.

## Dusk, Your Eyes

open
soft grinning
flash

then
all of the colors
in a pasture of fresh fallen snow.

# Willow Bed

discarded slippers / open window
tangled braid / shimmer field

push open the door / rush of empty
day stretches out, trembles & bends


damp harvest, low thrum


piercing mineral / cold swamp
blurred horizon, many tiny eyes

the thick of forest.
Step outside, barefoot

frost burning / soft arches
carry an empty basket, confusion

falling away

breathing.

# Hidden

in the woods
the first unfurl

hearty patch
of vibrant quiet.

## Signs

Worth & value
are measured now
     in exchanges of genuine smiles with our eyes,
or the crocuses returning, milky & sharp in the mud.
     A small tree still upright after the last winter storm,
a laugh sounding out from the neighbor's house
     like bells.

# & Suddenly

welcomed by overnight mud.
Fat red robins in graying mist.
An almost warm, ripe wind.
Phoebes flitting in the dark stand of pines
between shadowy shapes
who lean against each other
with arms outstretched.

Hill swept gentle & the smell of freshly split wood.

Malaise resists
seasons, healing.
I am holding on
to my winter.

What would it mean instead,        what responsibility,
what courage,
to feel well again?

Spring ephemerals are designed
for this heartiness

immunity, bitter nourishment
sting & kick, sour & grit.

I know loss.
How we cling to our sufferings,
protected there,
make meaning & identity out of our grief.

\* \* \* \* \* \* \* \*

Emerging in a slow, long walk in the rain.
Water sounding against raincoat

boots on yielding earth.
Sighs, white flags of steam.
Nettles, young fiddlehead & trillium

for whom I bend down, chest now in the mud
for a hint of its breathy, lemony scent.


It happens then                among & in spite of myself —

in the silky, Apriled soak
                              forebodings
                              fear of letting my winter go


melting to their singing     so pure an opening, & suddenly,  Spring.

# Overgrown

Before the lawn is mowed
a constellation emerges

in the not-yet-sweet green
in the-nearly-warm air

milky manes, serrated edges
slippery with night

It is time                    begin again.
It is time                    step into the light.

## Señora's Roses

54th Street slices through
the pain & down
into the dirty river
edge of noise
I wobble along
hurting, carefully,
between puddles & traffic.
Sirens rise & fall
through the wet slosh
in the street, on roofs.
Mask, scarf, hat, damp
shoulders hunched forward
lungs, small pink wings, beating.
Slow walk around the block.
Moving slow enough to notice her
for the first time
in her faded house dress & polka-
dotted hair wrap, thin slippers
slick with mist,
bent over golden
blooming buds,
her mouth deep in their folds
murmuring, something wrinkled & song-like.

## Spell for a Slower Life

I do not want the excuse
of sickness

to need the reason
of illness

I do not want to be forced
by poor health.

I do not want
the excuse of sickness

to need
the reason of illness

to be forced
by poor health

to have twenty eight hours
listening & quiet.

\* \* \*

Go outside after a dizzying rain
& lean down

watch the way the tall grasses
catch pieces of day

smell the earth sparkle
fill lungs, blood

go in, lay down again
& dream

of the sweetness
between soil & sky.

# Stranger

Restless in the day filled swell, a rush of energy like heat is moving
through the city. The world is alive with birds, bells
full & louder than I remember. Nearing them
on the fixed sidewalk, already early sun shine
shines a-blur. & underneath, this small wonder (glows).
Taut, their strange body hearth sparks close
even as we tilt ourselves away, the tight narrow
between our passing;   electric.
I'm not surprised to be scared, shocked
by their proximity — I mean, after all this
time. A stranger's fleeting cologne.
Their sweating crease of forehead.
Their sloping, laden undereye,
watery shoreside, daring to glance
at me, quick & bold. But most of all
their unhindered,  their actual,
their rose thistle mouth
so suddenly near, & bright.
    —unmasked, their whole face now
turning, lands
all unknown teeth & laugh wrinkles.
Forgotten reddening light
swells / then passes over me
a warm familiar, unfamiliar croon
brief imprint                that stirs.

## Salted Water

Evening, & a yawn
stretches over the roofs of this place.
New leaves, shy at first
tremble electric & almost pink
reach, purring with breath. Sometimes,
prayers don't look like we expect them to.
A night at first a day
drained & pale, casts its net
out to a sea of sleep
then lingers, sparkling
with all the darkness.

# Living

Lighting up her cheeks, first
shy, then gaining, blushing apricot,
torch, lava baring wild carnival
as small teeth show
flash of minnow, acropolis.

Slowly, soon, surprised
limbs, as if loosening
a run downhill

our shared laughter spreads,
flushes fluorescent

then surging, buoys
genuine, ripples through us

like last night's rain.

Lightly, lightly, light (ly).


When was it last, we could be as soft as this?


Circling,               a yellow bird in a clean sky.

# Surviving

Heat like this, where everything swells
where it becomes a choiceless choice, moving slower.

The neighbors open the fire hydrant on 54th Street
& the concrete steams. I want to shriek & play

in the arc of children's laughter, but I'm too tired.
Not minding that my bag & hair get wet,

I walk back & forth instead, through
the rainbow spray, smiling.

Returning hours later, when it is night, I enter
by familiar smell:

clean laundry, tacos, & mop water, limes.
Tank tops & Bachata in the damp night,

plastic cups of sticky liquor & soda, the tang of cooking meat
hanging low. A dropped watermelon split open on the sidewalk,

hot pink & seedless. Reggaeton base, gravely & thick.
Heaving families splayed out on stoops,

spilling over their plastic chairs & out into the street.
Children soaked, shouting, weaving between legs,

clutching tiny yellow water guns. On 6th Avenue
I pass two men helping another man towards an ambulance.

He is stooped over & stumbling, his eyes completely closed.
Beneath red flashing, the graying paramedic, snapping gum

& tilted forward by his heavy, muscled shoulders. "How much
did he have to drink today?" There is a sudden tenderness then,

in the quiet pause after he asks. Not politeness, exactly, but humility.
Three men gathered around a fourth, who is barely standing,

leaning against them with his full, human
weight. On all of their faces, the sting of a life.

Their stillness is cut, soon & suddenly,
by the high, picante whistle of a child's yell, a child

tugging at their mother's long braid as she thrusts a cart forward,
piled full with cans for deposit. Moving from beneath the street lamps,

shimmering, another child runs ahead of them, fat & jubilant.
A man is trailing him, calling out playfully

while pushing a stack of boxes on wheels,
running past us, rattling plastic, filling

the street with new sound. I follow them until the mural
of the uprising, then turn down 54th Street again.

The pavement is still wet from the open
fire hydrant & I can still feel heat through my sandals.

Hot & wet & tingle & night
through the street & dirty water,

crossing it slowly as if it's a river, lifting
my dress above my knees &

peering into the lit, open windows of other people's apartments
delighted by glimpses of their inside lives.

So this is the world, I think. So this is the world, as if I am not in it.
How beautiful it is.

& yet, how good —
to still be here, to have survived.

# Turning

amber, our front stoop
bronzed by gilded evening.
Patina of day
that shines our street

slow waters / thickets of sparks
               we risk entering

eyefuls of bitter marigold luz
round around persimmon yawn
wide lawn, jungle, dense & dewy
boombox base & lightning bug flick
alphabet limbs tangle salt, sweat, stink.
Lick sloppy lemon summer ice, drip
sticky, laughing sparkle touch
mouth
pour exquisite sheen
heat
melted by vibraphones, breeze
               a perfumed zodiac haze.


Our bodies, as they are.

# Closer

A man on Prince Street in a wide brimmed hat    sits on a milk crate
in front of a boarded up storefront          painted over
to be a field of purple clover     & plays the cello, sweating.

Plum pit, flies, hot metal, rotting trash
dead lilacs, linden pollen, people passing by
their arms hunched, or like branches, hang        thick with leaves

some glance
some do not

his fingers shake out aching from the strings
his jaw is a promise.

What I am trying to show you
is that I love this broken world.

There is ferocity
there is bravery that shocks me.

At times, we live so small

until a loss or disaster, a storm,
a sudden goodbye, or sometimes a stranger
reminds us what is outside of our tiny places

& we break open again.

## Returned

Hemlock sap
honeydew
moonriver
this wetted
green, again.
Hey,
I can learn

imperfect holiness.
I can learn this

dappled afternoon
& we, well enough
to stand
long legged

at the familiar
wooded entrance,

I have never been
so thankful.

# NOTES

The epigraph is from Anna Akhmatova's "A land not mine, still", as translated by Jane Kenyon.

"I Am Not Ready, Yet" is inspired by two poems of similar titles, one by Aracelis Girmay & one by Joy Harjo, respectively.

In "From A Still Place", the line *"all that appears to be taken / is still here"* borrows & alters language from Nayirrah Waheed's poem, "root | immortal".

In "Thankyou", the line, *"just like my mother I have longed to be / what I already am"* is inspired by a line from Esther Lin's poem, "La Traviata".

In "Surviving" the line, *"So this is the world, as if I am not in it"*, borrows & alters language from Mary Oliver's poem, "October".

"Glint" is dedicated to Don Rubén, with love.

# ACKNOWLEDGMENTS

My appreciation goes to the editors of the following publications, who published poems from this book, sometimes in earlier forms:

*Adult Groceries:* "Returned"
*Amethyst Review:* "Thankyou"
*Another New Calligraphy:* "Empty Empty / I Am Not Ready, Yet / This Bed / Willow Bed"
*Illuminations:* "Daybed / Letter From My Lung To My Legs"
*Impostor, a Poetry Journal:* "This Practice"
*No, Dear:* "Surviving"
*Rogue Agent Journal:* "Dew & Dirt"
*Roi Faineant Press:* "Green"
*Thimble Literary Magazine:* "Savored"
*Vagabond City Poetry:* "Being Ill"
*West Trestle Review:* "Glimmerers"
*Willows Wept Review:* "A Time"

# A NOTE FROM THE AUTHOR

My deep thanks to friends, family, fellow poets, advocates, alternative medical practitioners, counselors, & teachers who partnered with me through the times of illness, diagnosis, treatment, recovery & convalescence. To you, my heart & humbleness. Thank you to the staff at Cornerstone Press for such a collaborative and meaningful publication experience; Dr. Ross K. Tangedal, Ellie Atkinson, Paige Biever, Allison Lange, Sam Bjork and Sophie McPherson—a true privilege. Appreciation to Holly Wren Spaulding, Sophie Wood, & the Joy Sparks triage for their close readings, as well as Shira Erlichman, the In Surreal Life community, and my many poet comrades for prompts, encouragement, & support of this manuscript. An honor. To Soraya; romance, companionship & care unconditionally offered, my beloved devotion. For the attendance of ancestors, & that of poetry, always the meaning-maker, my sincere dedication. To you, reader, this would not be an offering without you. Thank you. To you who is, or has been, or will be changed by illness, by sickness, & by mortality—I accompany you. We are in cohort, in constellation. My profound gratitude goes to the nurses at the TB clinic of Springfield, MA, & to Dr. Sybille Liautaud, who kept me alive & got me Tuberculosis free with her tenacity & ingenuity during 2020-2022. Tuberculosis remains the world's leading infectious disease killer in 2025. There is a severe need for funding, research, development of treatment, freedom from stigma, & global Tuberculosis awareness. Many are working hard on this. To learn more about TB advocacy from TB survivors: www.wearetb.com

Aiyana Masla is the author of the chapbook *Stone Fruit* (2020). Her poems and art have been featured in the *West Trestle Review, For the Wild, Rogue Agent Journal, Willows Wept Review, Deluge Journal, Wildness, Elysium Review,* and other collections or anthologies. She was born in the middle of August, and works (plays) interdisciplinarily as an artist and educator. More of her work can be found at www.AiyanaMasla.com

www.ingramcontent.com/pod-product-compliance
Lightning Source LLC
Chambersburg PA
CBHW031243120626
46545CB00007B/2631